Back in Boley
A story based on true events in this all-colored midwestern town during the early 1900's
by S.P. Jennifer

ISBN 978-0-7414-3464-7

Published by:

INFINITY
PUBLISHING.COM

1094 New DeHaven Street, Suite 100
West Conshohocken, PA 19428-2713
Info@buybooksontheweb.com
www.buybooksontheweb.com
Toll-free (877) BUY BOOK
Local Phone (610) 941-9999
Fax (610) 941-9959

Printed in the United States of America

Published February 2015

Contents

Foreword

Back in Boley is a story based on true family accounts, and records from that time, of life in this "gem of all colored towns." This was how Booker T. Washington referred to the town after his visit there. Names have been changed but the written events are well documented. Readers will find themselves refreshed by continuing the historical study and reading of African American tenacity, triumphs and struggles for preservation, self determination, and human dignity.

Chapter 1--Faces to the Enemy

Go west, young man, was more than a catchy slogan for manifest destiny—for the colored, battle worn soldier, it was his SOS reply, and a rallying cry for freedom. It was, for anyone, who could recognize in its embedded code, the ticket out of the oppressive shackles of slavery and the way to take hold of a piece of the rock of financial independence. It would be a fitting tribute to those fighting men, who would give the last full measure of devotion to have bequeathed on them and their loved ones, a promised 40 acres and a mule.

On July 17, 1863, this hope for a new liberty would not be fulfilled for many of the colored soldiers lined up for the battle of Honey Springs, Oklahoma. At this time, Oklahoma was Indian territory, considered a fair prize for both the Union and Confederate armies. Both sides were confident that they could obtain a victory for this western territory.

US Major General James Blunt had marched his men all night. The Camden Expedition, planned ostensibly for establishing a northern presence in the south, was proving more elusive by the day. The arid land proved difficult for foraging, and several Native American tribes, the Choctaw and Chickasaw, in particular, had joined allegiance with the confederate army. At ten in the morning, the Battle of Honey Springs, later dubbed the Gettysburg of the West, began in earnest. The 1st Kansas Colored unit was ordered to charge the rebel artillery lines breastwork. The Confederate line, though hit hard, did not waiver. The 1st Kansas Colored lost their colonel in the heat of battle, but determinedly maintained their position. They had committed to memory his rallying words to them before the battle engaged. He reminded them that this was a "holy war" they were fighting, one that would give freedom to their children and their children's children. He emboldened them to show courage and to let the enemy know that they fought as brave disciplined men. Whether they lived or died, they would fight with their faces toward the enemy, and the nation would read the reports that their conduct was brave and disciplined. They persisted with small arms fire, as the battle raged on for several hours. During a brief moment of cease-fire, the demons of war began their work of confusion. The Union's Indian Home Guard unit found themselves in a pall of smoke and continued to wander into unprotected no man's land. A Union officer yelled for them to get back into guarded position. The always aggressive Texan unit, thought they had heard the Union call retreat. They leaped from their protective breastwork, with a howling rebel yell and began to charge what they thought were retreating Union army soldiers. They discovered, instead, the tenacious 1st Kansas Colored, who under forage cover, had maintained their position, and surprised the Texas unit with a barrage of fire at point-blank range. The enemy flag fell for a moment, and was then hoisted up again by a Texan soldier. Another volley of fire from the 1st Kansas buckled the rebel line and crumbled the charge. Confederate Brig. Gen Douglas Cooper summonsed a retreat to save remaining forces. Union forces pursued until both sides reached the Honey Springs depot. Confederates last line of defense was broken at this point. Through this victory, the Union gained control of Indian territory. There was no longer the need to debate which army ruled the west. Honey Springs proved to be a storehouse for Confederate supplies and quite a bounty for the Union. A cache of shackles was found, that it was said would have been used to take the colored soldiers back as slaves. Colored soldiers could count on incessant reminders of why they were fighting this war. These morbid declarations of inhumanity only steeled the colored soldiers determination to win this war and their freedom with it. The battle at Honey Springs was unique in that it was the first time colored and Indian soldiers outnumbered white soldiers on the battlefield. It proved to be a significant lode for opinions regarding the ability of colored soldiers. It decidedly proved the worth and necessity of utilizing the colored soldier to help end the worst bloodletting the nation had ever experienced.

Eva, precocious Eva, taught this history with fire and brimstone, and rarely lost a student in the process. They found her youthful zeal captivating, and trusted instruction from her. Her charges were honored when she treated them to her grandfather's Civil War discharge papers.

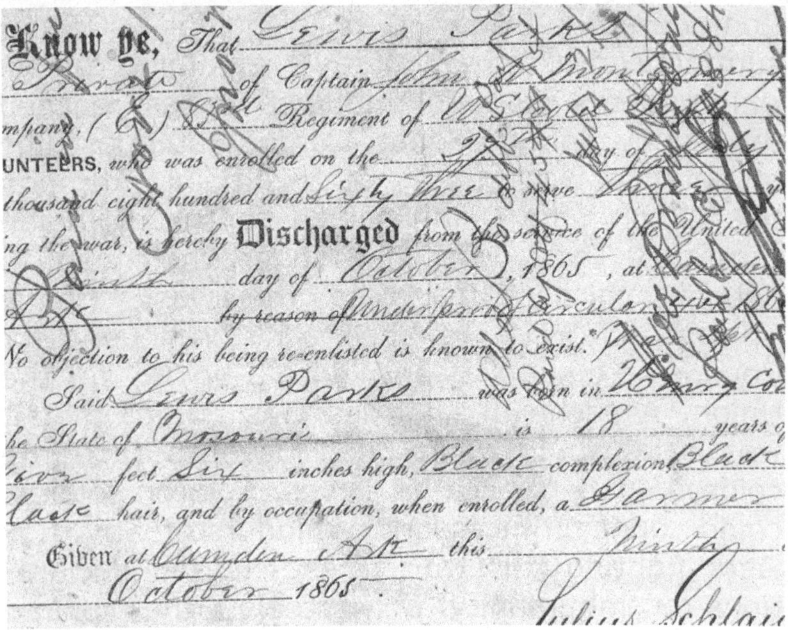
Know Ye, That Lewis Parks
Private of Captain John ... Montgomery
mpany, (G) ... Regiment of U.S. ...
UNTEERS, who was enrolled on the 27 day of ...
thousand eight hundred and Sixty Three to serve ...
ng the war, is hereby Discharged from the service of the United
Ninth day of October, 1865, at ...
Ark by reason of ...
No objection to his being re-enlisted is known to exist.
Said Lewis Parks was born in ... Co
he State of Missouri is 18 years o
Five feet Six inches high, Black complexion, Black
Black hair, and by occupation, when enrolled, a Farmer
Given at Camden Ark this Ninth
October 1865.

Students were reminded to take notes dutifully as she taught, and many of the students had relatives who had participated in the Oklahoman Battle of Honey Springs. Students were elevated and integrated into the history of their town, Boley. These history lessons engendered a strong sense of pride, having the knowledge colored people from their town had played in shaping the history of the nation. Miss Eva informed them about several were at least 29 all Negro towns during the time this was stated, including the Tulsa colored town district, Greenwood, designated as the Negro Wall Street. Boley considered herself "the gem of colored towns." She, alone felt the call to sparkle like none other.

Preparations for the town's biggest event, the 101 Ranch Cowboy Rodeo show was underway. Friends, family, strangers packed the town to partake of the festivities. Cowboys, unaccustomed to walking, clopped the streets, enjoying the admiration of the townsfolk. They were the heroes of the town, whose strength and determination inspired all who gazed upon them. To top this all off, Boley was the town selected as the backdrop for famous Negro cowboy Bill Pickett, and the movie in which he would star—*Crimson Skull*. The air was charged in fanciful anticipation of his arrival. A young boy, hawking the ***Boley Progress***, helped spread the news. It was an exciting time for the town. Jim "Soda Pop" Washington was all smiles. Extra orders of soda pop were coming in steadily, and the Boley Carbonated Soda Works was in the money. Elmer's Boots and Saddlry preached, "Heeling of Boots, Saving of Soles, and even Dyeing for You." Hotels were booked for the week and many would just as soon rent a room in one of the townfolks home if needed. That's the kind of place Boley had become. Never was there a discouraging word, or **No Negroes Allowed** signs to worry about. Not even huge bales of cotton being unloaded from a nearby dock could stir up slavery's memory. This cotton was owned by a prosperous Negro other battles they would need to study for th final exam on the Civil War. They would need know the differences in remuneration of t colored soldier versus the white soldier a some of the battle locations and strategi They would later come to realize the importan of these lessons in preparing them for t struggles and blessings that lay ahead for the in the town of Boley. For now, the ringing b signaled a truce from it all. Planning for nov centered around Trulove's Burger shop, ar who socially merited the window seat.

It was springtime in the west, different i Oklahoma from any other season in the country It meant violent storms and gentle breeze rolling over prairie grass plains. Oklahoma' designation as tornado alley only stoked th fierce determination of those independent fierce-spirited settlers who deemed it home Being a Boley native meant even more. It wa founded upon the time honored tradition in the west of gambling, with the stakes set by twc railroad men. One, certain that given the opportunity, colored folks could fare as well as any white man in self-determination. The other, just as sure that colored folks would always need the support of white men to survive. Boley folks were bound and determined to show anyone how industrious and prosperous they could be. And show, they did. Booker T. Washington's visit to the town inspired him to pronounce the town, "the most enterprising and in many ways the most interesting of the Negro towns." This was no idle compliment. There businessman, and buyers were swarming around it like bees to sweet honey. On Main Street, a stately gentleman steps from the pharmacy front, and holds his jaw, while feigning his way past the Candy Kitchen. A youthful schoolboy lands in front of a young couple and gets his "pants ironed" for his indiscretion. Signs of life in Boley abounded this particular spring.

Boley High students romped their way to Trulove's burger shop and filled most of the seats with orders ready. The Boley Bears were dominating the other local schools with their game skills and every eligible player was using the odds to benefit off court dalliances. Like the lyrics of the state song, the winds of freedom were blowing freely.

Chapter 2--Remember Poison Springs!

"That bull's eyes are as red as hot coals," Bill warned! "He's madder than a hornet and fixed to ram somebody!" It was preliminaries for the Miller Brothers 101 Wild West show. It was doing its job of weeding out only those cowboys good enough for final competition. Wham! That cowboy needed a clown lickety-split fast. The bull steamed straightway for his prize. A duck honk distracted the wild beast long enough for attendants to drag the bruised body from harms way. Wiley the clown, did not fare as well. His body was thrown by the bull over its head, and he partially feigned death. "Get up! Get up!" Two young boys shouted. "He's charging back for you," they yelled! Peeking through a slatted fence they could partially spy the drama unfold. Suddenly, firm hands attached themselves to both the boys shoulders. Startled, they turned to face Mr. Askew, the town truant officer. "You boys familiar with school hours around here," he quipped. The boys managed to stammer an affirmative, but bravely tried to petition for just a few minutes more to witness the legendary

"Dusky Demon", Bill Pickett. They were assured that there was no way under God's green earth that Bill Pickett would not make finals and they could witness his skills during the weekend like other smart schoolboys. He admonished them that getting a truant ticket would surely **guarUntee** that they would be punished and miss the show. They dragged their way back to school and slinked to their desk just as Miss Eva was starting history. "Tardiness, is the height of impropriety," she quipped. "You can tell me all about it during your recess time." She promptly proceeded to the Battle at Jenkins Ferry, Arkansas and the role of the colored soldiers there.

When the smoke cleared, she earnestly began, men of the colored troops from the 1st and 2nd Colored Kansas Infantry had given, in the words of President Lincoln, the last full measure of devotion.

For the first time, orders had been given for a colored unit to charge a rebel artillery. Each soldier knew what was at stake. Show valor at all costs, or henceforth forfeit another opportunity to prove that freedom was colorblind and worth fighting for. Not one soldier would forget to avenge the memories of comrades previously massacred at Poison Springs. Confederate officials had made it policy to kill all Union officers and to make all colored soldiers slaves if captured. The ravages of war however, further stoked mans inhumanity to man, and every colored soldier captured at Poison Springs was mercilessly slaughtered on the spot. Colored troops were outnumbered 10

to 1 and were slaughtered and butchered rather than taken as prisoners of war. The sheer horror of witnessing fellow brothers being slain was fresh in their memories this day. The 1st Kansas Colored lost nearly one half its numbers at Poison Springs.

Before the battle commenced, a Union officer, one General Rice, was not familiar with colored troops on the battlefield and promptly asked for their removal stating "They won't fight." Union officer Crawford, familiar with the sacrifices made by these colored soldiers at Poison Springs, in non-Christian terms, emphatically persuaded otherwise. General Rice was out to prove his point, however and reluctantly countered by sending the colored troops to the front lines to replace the 15th Indiana. For two hours the colored troops "engaged the enemy in earnest deadly conflict." The masterful eye of Union colonel Crawford surveyed the need to silence the rebel artillery and determined upon its capture to obtain a Union victory. Union General Rice was still unpersuaded to attempt a charge on the rebels by colored troops. He decided that only when his flank force had commenced cheering their success on the field would colored soldiers then be permitted to charge on the rebels. Well, Union officer Crawford heard cheering, but not from the Union side. Nevertheless, cheering was cheering, and he gave orders for the colored troops to fix bayonets and charge! Colored troops found themselves facing three times their own number, still they dashed upon the open field toward the rebel battery. The contest was

severe. Colored troops steeled themselves for the deadly work by exclaiming—"Remember Poison Springs!" The colored troops hurled a destructive reign of terror on the rebels that day. Most of the attending officers had their horses shot out from under them. The men of the 2nd charged the rebel battery and successfully captured it. One hundred and fifty rebels were killed or mortally wounded. This time, a higher moral ground was also taken, and the captured rebel soldiers were taken as prisoners. It was in striking contrast to the treatment colored soldiers had received at Poison Springs. Some wounded Union colored soldiers still needed to be left behind for treatment. This posed a dilemma for the Union officer. He knew about rebel sentiment toward colored soldiers, but needed to press on for Fort Smith. He admonished a rebel Lieutenant that "if they could afford to murder our colored prisoners to gratify their fiendish dispositions and passions, the responsibility of commensurate retaliation, to bring them to a sense of justice, was also their own." The confidence shown to the rebel prisoners, however, was to no avail. Not long after the Union officer left, a Confederate soldier from Texas killed nine of the wounded men from the 2nd colored, in the presence of his officers. From this massacre and other disappointments, doubt arose over the need for this expedition. Many good men had been killed to obtain questionable advantage. Dutifully, however, the Union forces continued their march back to Fort Smith. Many men marched shoeless, and with a loaf of bread as

rations for seven days. A piece of hard tack or an ear of corn commanded the exorbitant price of from one to five dollars and their was many a starving mule who gave of his meal for the exchange.

Confederate forces near Fort Smith had expected a Union defeat at Jenkins Ferry, and were eagerly anticipating the arrival of their victorious comrades. Anxious rebel sympathizers were receiving regular reports of the armies approach. Their bridled joy would soon to be spent on rousing cheers for their returning heroes. But what to their "mortification and grief should appear, not the dear southern army with flying colors and music playing, but the colored brigade, marching through the main streets to the joy and delight of only the loyal citizens. Sorrow and tears belonged to the disloyal, to which there were not a few."

The conduct of these brave soldiers proved to even the most skeptical, the practicability of mustering into service a large force of them. It was realized then..."Men good enough to save their country—were good enough to enjoy all the blessings and privileges which the government confers on any class of her citizens." Colored soldiers knew this battle was a turning point in the war. This was the moral ground they had been fighting for all along. Their mission, along with their brothers who had fought at Honey Springs, Oklahoma, Fort Wagner, South Carolina, Jenkins Ferry, Arkansas and countless other places in this Civil War, had been accomplished.

Miss Eva summarized that the sacrifices made by these men should make Boley residents feel nothing but respect and pride for them. These were the men that made the town possible for them. She enjoined her students to continue the legacy of fierce courage and determination, for which those colored soldiers so bravely fought. Students would research one of the soldiers who fought in the colored units and write a report about their contribution which hastened the end of a long and bloody Civil War. She admonished none to want for information, since they had been given several pages of notes. As an aside she noted that in Oklahoma, the land of the red people, one of the last confederate generals to surrender was Brigadier General, Stand Watie, a Cherokee Indian.

Miss Eva was no less a taskmaster than any war general, and dismissed her students to the charge at hand. Where in Boley, would one find a musing Civil War mentor?

Chapter 3--Breath of Freedom

Some decades ago, men who would be inspired by Boley were created in this fashion.

There was Sam, who winced for his wife and muffled a prayer for her, as she dragged her limp, bruised body to the splintered wooden porch. His heart pounded defiantly in defense for her, but it too, found the confines of its cage. He desperately searched for his manhood against this bold affront to it. He heard Boss cackle; Tell Sam he can have any of the leftovers," as he crept back to the big house. Sam went to Belle, but he dared not touch her. These assaults to her body and soul would take months of shunning from any man, even her own husband. He understood, and hurt too. He lay dazed with her, from the shock of knowing he could do little to protect her. He endured with her, time and again, becoming a little more numb each time. And still, he had not made good on his promise to her that they would leave this plantation for a better place to live.

A son, born months later, bore witness to his daddy's absent lineage. Glaring green eyes stared at him in disbelief while nestling in Sam's arms. He would adopt him as his own and teach him to keep the secret well. After all, his mother had several fair skinned relatives, whose family ties were questionable, he should fare well. Yes, he would love and raise him as his own, before the ascent of guileless truth would arise and overtake his sensibilities against the child. Boss, Mr. Ed, would also see to it that baby William would have most of his needs met. At least those that money could buy. He resented accepting anything from ruthless Ed, but he knew Belles blood also belonged to the boy. That was his only salvation.

Belle grew colder and more withdrawn. Her body was not her own, and dying while living was the only way she knew to cope with the constant pain. Her daily toiling and incessant scrubbing did little to relieve her anguish or ease her fears of renewed attacks on her body. Still, she labored on, caring for her family dutifully and tending to their needs as best she could.

Sam came in from the fields one particularly bright spring morning with a flyer in his hand. Always curious about reading, Belle reached for the paper to Sam's delight. He pulled back from her advances, which only provoked her interest all the more. Sam playfully teased her once again and told her the information was for "men folk" only. She straightened her countenance and directed him to "be a man" and give her the letter. She could scarcely hide her interest in its contents. It announced a fair would be arriving in town soon, and it would be a gay time for all. Belle knew she would be presenting her best peach cobbler, and was ruminating about its

Come when the year's first blossom blows,
Come when the summer gleams and glows,
Come with the winter's drifting snows,
And you are welcome, welcome.

He was always vulnerable to her touch, and st then she gently embraced him. Her tender uch breached his well of uncertainties, and at night he knew her well. Enraptured, they ad found the way of escape and floated rough the night. Once again, their love had voked a weapon song, and kept out the war of e world against them.

Belle worked through the numbered days ith ease. She had a sense of purpose and was etermined that she would present the best—e best man—the best peach cobbler—the best ess the town had ever seen on a colored ervant woman. These proved to be another ay of escape for her and she wrapped herself its secrecy. Sam was working even longer ours now. He was determined that Belle have at new dress, and he vowed that it would be ers and not some creditors. Still, she missed m and though she could handle a Remington, o, she nervously longed to be wrapped in the rong shoulders of his protection.

The day of the fair came none too soon. am seemed entranced by his wife, framed in e bedroom door. She was a vision of veliness to him in that dress. It had been ome time since she had gussied herself so. He ld her it would suit him just fine if they were a tle late for the fair. But Belle was ready to avor every moment, and William was crying to

secret contents, when Sam gently s
from behind. Sure do wish I didn't
alone, but it's just too busy around
you go." he joked. Belle insisted t
there would be no need for him to r
if he didn't bring her with him to the
just the assurance Sam needed to
with a gift for just such an occasion.
a bow-wrapped package behind the
As she slowly opened it, a large n
square of shantung fabric greeted h
face. She knew just what dress
design and a forgotten wellspr
overtook her. Sam told her she w
belle of the fair, which further i
vision.

Now, there was so much to do!
days left to complete her task
purpose, was what she desired. Nov
some purpose to her days.

That night, she thought she coul
Sam's touch was no longer an affror
he entreated her with poetry.
assurance he began;

You are sweet, O Love, dear Lov
You are soft as the nesting dove.
Come to my heart and bring it re
As the bird flies home to its welc

Come when my heart is full of gr
Or when my heart is merry;
Come with the falling of the leaf
Or with the redd'ning cherry

be included, too. So, everything was packed in the wagon and it was off to the fair.

Friends had come from near and far for this social event. It was not often that hard working folks like these could take time from demanding field work to attend to pure fun and relaxation. Most came dressed in their Sunday best, ready to stroll and strut before long lost neighbors and friends. Judges, too, were eyed from head to toe, to detect any hint of selected prize winners. Two ladies were found quarreling about a dish entry and suspected recipe snooping, when one of the judges allayed their fears. He assured them that all judging had been completed some time ago. Judges were simply enjoying the leftovers and waiting to announce the prize winners. A renewed sense of fellowship ensued, and folks milled around for the announced winners. Belle had no consciousness of guilt for the sole desire of the blue ribbon decorating her deserving hand and home. Many, in particular those not participating, scoffed at such justifications of self worth. But, the announcement of her name referred to, as a winner no less, sent springs of suppressed hope within her. This bright day would go a long way to sustain her life efforts. She well-nigh floated to the stand for her prize. The shantung dress held her well, as she carouseled with Sam. She giddily claimed her prize and proceeded through the fair with the admiration of many and the respect of those who had participated devoutly.

Bumps and jolts from the wagon ride home, that usually taunted their work-weary bones, only rocked them peacefully this night. It had been a good day, and every moment was to be savored. The harsh realities of field life would be back too soon, they knew. And so they were determined to enjoy every moment of the day and this glorious expansive starry night.

Some days later, Belle awoke with a dizzying sickness that kept her in bed. Sam became more alarmed as the sickness lingered and went for help. To Sam's relief, it was discovered that Belle was not suffering from any near death ailment as he believed. She was with child. An event that was meant for the best sentiments, only brought fear and thoughts of dread. Sam had done all he could possibly do to contain his anger toward Boss Ed, but this time he vowed it would be his vengeance and not the Lord's, that would remedy any broken paternal lines, that tormented him so. This child, unlike William, did not struggle within her. She would gently nudge her stomach often to obtain a response. The child was living gently and peacefully inside her and rarely allowed his presence to be known. How strange, Belle thought, of this small person's nature.

Stranger still, was the day of his birth. A storm had brewed that produced one of the worst nor'easters in a while. A howling scream was not from the wind or loss of the roof, but the sounds of life from a new born baby boy. It was an unusually loud cry that seemed to foretell the events of his future as William's brother, Eli. This time, true celebration was in order as Sam and Belle's worst fears were not realized. Belle discovered that the life within her belonged to her and her beloved Sam only.

Not unlike Jacob and Esau of old, the brothers soon grew to discover the distance between them. Belle was determined that William would always feel like a member of the family, without exception. Sam, however, wanted Eli between his loins when the family portrait was taken. In the photo everyone was touching one another except William. He stood slightly off to the side. His mother never noticed this slight until after the photo was placed on the mantle. Eli had also begun to nurture some slights of his own. The ordained pecking order of the first born was interpreted by him as favoritism. It seemed that William would get most things he asked for, even with the meager funds of the family. Boss Ed had seen to it that William received a gold piece on his 16th birthday, telling him something about being a man and buying up life's pleasures. Eli discovered the coin in William's privy box and made good use of it, he thought, at the merchandise store. William, after several inquiries, determined the pilferer to be none other than Eli. He lit into Eli with a pent up fury usually reserved for his class rivals. Eli fought back, but tried to come from behind with an insult that forever changed his brother's relationship with him. He told William that he could prove to him that he was really white. William's worse thoughts were now vocalized and he thought he would silence his brother forever from those same echoes that resounded constantly within him. Sam appeared just in time to come between them as William jabbed the air. The damage had been done. William felt officially branded as the family outcast. Belle did all she could to comfort him, but he turned cold and distant from them, and would not be solaced. He would find a way to leave this place called home, forever. Some time later, to his great relief, he would accept the call from Uncle Sam and adopt him as his new family member.

William served his country honorably, as a war historical correspondent. He had obtained the rank of Sergeant Major and would make sure a letter back to the family, especially to Eli, made this clear.

His unit posed before the bombed out Chateau de Cherhery, in Argonne, France. Another photo of him and his all colored unit standing in front of a captured gunnery made William, his mother wrote, a home town hero. He was determined however, to make good on his vow to make himself a new home.

Hopes of heroes welcomes and equality, were soon dashed upon William's return home, when he learned that some of America's best colored soldiers had been lynched in uniform by jealous white mobs. He received ambiguous responses also, but the hard fought freedom he had helped to forge, pressed heavily upon him. He would no longer accept second-class citizenship after his first class performance defending those unalienable rights. Somewhere William heard the cry to go west, and he was still young enough to believe its promise of hope and freedom. Perhaps there was a place where he could realize all the dreams and nascent aspirations that were ripe within him. The west, then, would be the place to fecundate them. He had heard about one town in particular that had established good order and was run entirely by colored folks. Had his ears deceived him? He had to find out for himself.

Next stooop, Muskogee! He heard the conductor exclaim. Half roused, he peered from the shaded window to get a view of his new surroundings. Arighting himself, he picked up his few possessions from his berth. Striding from the train, he managed a ride from a fellow whom he overheard talking about his destination as Boley. The stranger seemed curiously relieved to hear about another convert, wanting to stake a claim in the model town. With a slight chuckle, he shared with William that fools didn't suffer kindly in that town, and he'd better be knowing that right now. He inquired about the goods William would be bringing to the town, and acted much like the town's guardian angel. William's military service was what stilled his voice, though, and soon William found himself front and center on the town's main street. His driver insouciantly refused pay for the journey, assuring William that he was glad to help him get on his feet, and looking out for one another was the Boley way of doing things.

Looking about him, William saw a small bustling town, but this much was quite evident. Colored folks were in charge—everywhere. His eyes danced with delight at the many vignettes before him. There was a pharmacy where a colored man was handing a prescription to a man who was grimacing while holding his jaw; Two stout men, one with a watch in hand, stepped from the bank and drove from an awaiting Packard, gleaming with fresh wax. From the tailor's shop, a gentleman appeared, with attending brushes of his suit from its owner. Beautiful ladies abounded, one in particular who was departing from a department store tipped her hat to keep him from further partaking of her virtue. Entranced by her comeliness, he pursued her for some distance, until he was stirred to attend to the business at hand. This would entail the pursuit of honest means of employment in order to partake of such recreational diversions. He would have to prove himself worthy of "beauhood" for the likes of these ladies. That would be a quest worthy of the undertaking he surmised.

All the talk about Boley surely was well founded. This appeared to be the promised land he was seeking. He engaged his mind in all the possibilities. He knew what he wanted just then, and latent desires to take what he wanted would not subside. He had set his sights on success and that sweet ingénue who intrigued him. He would plan his work and work his plan, until he had achieved his desired purpose.

A bill, posted in a nearby store, announced a town meeting for "the purpose of permitting the operation of a train stop for Boley." Here, William figured, would be the place to meet the town's movers and shakers. The proprietor of a nearby hotel, aptly named Mrs. Hussel, directed him to an available room looking over Main Street. He slept peacefully, until awakened by the heady aroma of a freshly prepared home cooked meal.

He obtained directions to the town meeting from Mrs. Hussel, and proceeded to the largest building in Boley, the Masonic Temple. It was decision making time. Everyone knew that the life line of Boley, would be the efficient operation of a train stop, right through the town. Boley, however, was in competition with the nearby town of Castle, for this prestigious boon. As folks buzzed about the matter, a small group of distinguished gentlemen entered the room and commenced to call the meeting to order. Situated around a large oak table, Mayor Turner called up the matter of a train station for Boley. After some discussion about the situation, A white-haired gentleman raised his voice to speak, and a hush ensued across the room. Here was someone worth listening to, William thought. The gentleman's, one Mr. Clint Crawford, suggestion was that one of the town members should go to Castle and sit in on their meeting regarding the train stop. This way Boley could ascertain what they planned to offer. Whispers ensued, most defending a more altruistic means of business, a few intimating the gentleman's familiarity with this mode of operation, namely spying. Nevertheless it was decided by the unanimous vote from the town council that the idea was sound, and per Mr. Crawford's suggestion, he should well be the one to carry the plan out. The meeting adjourned until the necessary information was gathered, and the council decided to convene sometime later in the month to finalize a business plan.

William had managed to find his way across the room to make Mr. Crawford's acquaintance and was straightway befriended by the personable gent. William talked himself into a home cooked dinner and some family time with Mr. Crawford's brood, as he called it. After traveling some distance from the town, William wondered how a man so dedicated to the town had come to live so far from it. William's curiosity got the better of him and he dared to ask. Mr. Crawford said he and William had something in common, so he didn't mind answering the question at all. "You see William," he explained, "I'm somewhat of an outcast in this town, as you may have figured from the meeting tonight." William assured him that he saw quite a bit of respect given to him at the meeting that night. "However," Mr. Crawford continued, "folks around here said they weren't sure if I was white or whiter, and this town was going to be built by colored folks only. They said I could easily ruin the bet that was on, about this town. You see plenty of folks are wagering, including some big railroad tycoons, that colored folks don't know nothing about taking care of themselves like white folks. So, that's how Boley came about. We're sitting on top of a big old stack of odds against us, so I help out the best I can, knowing what side I belong on. I think the good Lord made folks that look like us, 'tweeners, maybe we're supposed to help make a bridge for white and colored folks to cross. We've had some of the humanity you get from being white, and we're also familiar with the injustices of being colored. But it seems folks like me just don't pass muster, overall, if you know what I mean." William knew exactly what he meant. He had been second guessed all his life about his color and race, there was no need to say another word about it. He would stack his chips with Boley, too. And find a way to beat the odds against him.

Mr. Crawford's house decorated the prairie field like the gilded ornament it was. There was a small orchard on one side and a carefully tended garden on the other. Beyond, in the distance, William could just make out the outline of tombstones outlining the evening sky. Mr. Crawford instructed William that he would need a wealth of talents to succeed in a prairie town like Boley. Hence, the fruit trees and the cemetery. There was even a flat strip of meadow land for prop planes to land. Mr. Crawford had already provided him with many lessons on successful business ownership. He, too, would learn to be wise and enterprising like his new-found mentor.

Through the screen door, a familiar scent wafted. Chicken-fried steak and gravy with fresh rolls infused the well dressed parlor room before him. Mr. Crawford had a wife as bountiful as he, and she graciously welcomed them to the living room. She was determined to fill any empty spot of William's that she could find, and ensured this with a generous dinner and for dessert, a heaping portion of her pecan pie. It was a wonderful meal, fit for a king, and made the welcoming to Boley all the sweeter. He questioned if life could get any better. The answer lightly knocked on the screen door and sauntered in.

Yes indeed, was the glorious response to his musings. There before him was the sweet young lady he had set his sights on earlier! Well, do tell, she cooed, Y'all having company for dinner with me in this frightful state of affairs. Surely she knew how divine she looked, William thought. Beauty on its best day couldn't touch her boundaries. Staring was all William could manage. Mr. Crawford, too, was enchanted with his delightsome daughter, and finally managed an introduction. William, this is my precious daughter, Eva. Mr. Crawford continued, regaling over all her many talents, not sensing that they had already met, and destiny had completed her duty. "It's a pleasure making your acquaintance, Miss Eva." William smiled. One more gaze into her eyes and he would have surely worn out his welcome, William thought. He shared with Mr. Crawford his plans to establish an ice plant in

Boley, which seemed an excellent idea to Mr. Crawford. He offered to bring up the idea for a loan opportunity before the bank board, of which he was a member. When William inquired about a lift back into town, another son, Chance, appeared, and was eager to drive William to town. Eva, too, seemed faintly interested in the handsome stranger, and offered to accompany him and Chance, but was reminded by her daddy of her "frightful state." She persistently offered Chance the opportunity for some company on the ride back, and to William's delight found himself in her company a while longer. He made small talk with Chance, and big strides into Eva's heart. From that night on, Mr. Crawford always made sure that his pubescent daughter was doggedly chaperoned on her night outings.

Chapter 4--Stake Out

The Boley town council had announced another meeting regarding the progress of obtaining a local train station for the town. New information would be shared on the outcome of a Boley train depot for its citizens. The excitement of Boley becoming a hub for more visitors and businesses was shaking the foundation of the town. Town folks crowded the hall to learn about the decision. As the meeting commenced, it became evident that Mr. Crawford had not steered the town wrong. Castle town's business plan was lacking in a few necessities, including a strong section gang. Boley's plan included trained ticket agents, telegraph operators, and a foreman. It had been decided by the Fort Smith Western Railroad that Boley would be the preferred railway stop! A thunderous round of applause greeted this news and folks were ecstatic to learn that possibly the world would now be arriving at Boley town. Not long after this, to the delight of many, colored leader Booker T. Washington would be one of many to ride in on the rails of the town to shower it with his blessings of prosperity and crown it as the gem of Negro towns. It appeared that Boley was on the rise and on the winning end of the gamble regarding its success.

Soon, more businesses and homebuyers, financed by the Farmers and Merchants Bank of Boley, established themselves in the town. The bank became known as one of the soundest in the southwest. Boley's population swelled, and made it the largest colored town in America. Perhaps it was now time to collect all bets and cash in on its well established reputation.

Being well known, during some of the nation's most desperate economic times, however, was a curse, as well as a boon. The west, even more so than the freshly sutured nation, was still a wild, untamed place, filled with men who took pleasure in their outlaw status. The nation found itself in the middle of the times that try men's souls, which times also found deluded defenders of the Lost Cause, still on the war path. Their new battle plan of Jim Crow, secretly enacted in smoke-filled, late night lodge meeting rooms, and woven into many western state constitutions, would be used to offset and resurrect the resounding loss of free slave labor. Oklahoma's constitution provided for the support of Jim Crow legislation by segregating its public facilities. It also banned interracial marriages, although the promise of Native American's land rights caused both Negroes and whites to ignore this order. Others simply blamed hunger and desperation as the enemies of their lost social graces and their misplaced salvation. The vast west proved big enough to run and hide from the long arm of the law, and run here they did.

Boley also found itself facing the backdraft of the flames from the nearby Tulsa race riots. The all colored district, known as Greenwood, had been burned to its base by white mobs, determined to rid the city of its "Negro Wall Street." Boley residents steeled themselves for any fallout from this conflagration; its men stood ready to defend their town to the death, and had established men with solid reputations as crack shots and veteran officers and soldiers within its ranks. Boley resident's worst fears were not realized during that marauding time in Oklahoma's history. But it strengthened the town's sense of purpose and need for self determination, amid one of the nations worst breakdowns in civil police protection and criminal enforcement.

Still, Boley's bank stood. Amidst an excess of crime and lawlessness, it stood. Its bank had not had a single robbery during one of the worst runs on bank robberies of its time. Most outlaws were affronted by anything virgin near their surroundings, especially untouched money. Boley's bank was the apple of many a bandits eye, and piqued by a rare few.

In that number, there was one bandit group, who thought themselves ready for the challenge. It was made up of one of the most notorious robbers of that day, Charles Arthur "Pretty Boy" Floyd. This group of desperados thought it time to stake out the town of Boley and test its mettle. After several stakeouts of the town, the group's leader, Pretty Boy, determined that the bank was too well maintained to rob and told the group to scrap plans of robbing it. It appeared the reputation of the Boley men had proceeded past them, right up to the nation's most notorious bandit. For several of Floyd's gang members, this admonition fell on deaf ears and they made clandestine plans to proceed with the bank robbery without him. Several had felt that Floyd's family ties in Oklahoma had softened him up, an emotion for which they had no use. Perhaps Floyd's dad, a Mason, had bargained with some of the Boley town members, to make its bank neutral ground. But for Floyd's gang, all was fair in love and bank robbing, and they would have nothing to do with such formal allegiances. Theirs was a brotherhood of bandits, with all the name implied. They barely stood for fair takes and splits, and many a time a bandit brother was lost, shot down, in that process. Even former Confederate ambusher, turned bank robber, Jesse James, lamented about the lack of camaraderie and trust among fellow thieves. He was betrayed by one from his posse and shot while in his trust. Undaunted by his hero's fate, it was well known that Pretty Boy was inspired by Jame's despotic deeds and was nurtured on stories of his history. Indeed, desperate times had produced some of the most desperate men that law enforcement had ever faced. And Pretty Boy, and his cohorts found many a friend and family member in Oklahoma, and the Cooksom Hills in particular, to be very endearing towards them when the law came bearing down.

Floyd's boys determined to go it alone in Boley, and continued to stake out the town and lay claim to its cache.

Negro bandit, Pete Glass, determined he would show Floyd how to rob a colored bank and set out to make his plans. He would bust things loose in Boley. His scheme included watching and waiting, as he called it, fueled by thoughts of "a never been touched bankroll." He would bide his time and learn the ways of Boley. His ultimate climactic lust for "the take" he would temporarily satisfy by gambling and nesting in the company of its pretty women. He never figured that the shrewd folks in Boley had also decided he, too, was one they had better keep an eye on.

Folks described summertime in Boley as hotter than hell's kitchen. For William, it was pure bliss. He had successfully managed financing for his ice company, and on this day, he was one of the most sought after men in town. He had a flair, he thought, for cooling folks down, especially the young ladies. He had long since set his mind on obtaining Eva's hand, but found some detours along the way before sparkin' with her. Before he knew it, he had acquired a whole plantation of admirers. It didn't take long for him to assess that none had the wit and charm of Eva. She was an honors student from nearby Langston College and excelled in discourse and lecture. This would *compliment* him well in the social circles he was eyeing. She also could play any sweet tune requested on the piano. There were so many choices, but few opportunities as the one provided by Eva. Her youth, most importantly her youth, would be his insurance of perpetual beauty in his midst, he surmised. She too, seemed attracted to his intelligence and charm. She dismissed the cunning calculations made in his conversations about her being such an asset to him. She was determined she needed to hear herself mentioned as more that just a column in his account book, but the heady emotions of his love could not sustain her reasoning. Fantastic ideas of being the "lady of the house" distracted her from such raw realism. When Mr. Crawford hinted that any son-in-law of his would partake of his gracious bounty and a bank board position as well—William took the bait, and directly proceeded to go. He asked Eva for her hand in marriage. Mr. Crawford had his reservations about William, but he had committed by oath to his lodge of finding new recruits to fill its waning ranks. William was eyed with promising potential for its membership. With no hint of collusion with her father, she blushed in dismay but managed to accept his proposal, just the same, that day.

A glorious wedding was planned, with only a few disappointed arrivals at the ceremony. Mr. Crawford spared no expense for his only daughter. A wedding gift of several acres of land finalized his approval of the couple. William felt he had come a long way since his plantation days. That night William pledged his loyalty to Eva, along with reassuring her that she would never have need of anything. It took Eva some time to realize that she had accepted his terms compromisingly. After all, he was thirteen years her senior, and she had so much still, to learn.

William began the lesson by gently teaching her through their honeymoon night.

A son birthed from this union arrived pale and blue. A haunting scream from Eva upon receiving the news filled the house. William appeared distant and numbed by the experience, it brought back painful memories of his mother's face after a day in Boss Ed's plantation house. He did not go in to soothe Eva's fears, but ran from the house and drove to the bank and began tediously arranging accounts receivable records. Like a newborn in need of a mother's first touch, Eva, too, had found herself neglected from a touch when she needed it most. She fell into a deep depression of which she was only mildly aware. It was months later, when she found out that she was with child again, that she ceased from the habit of daily sobbings.

She buoyed herself with thoughts of new life and miraculous giving—by her body and God's gift of motherhood. This child would be, she willed, and prepared in faith for all of its needs. Mr. Crawford came by to visit and noticed many domestic items missing from the house and inquired about its furnishings. Eva defended her husband by explaining that they were saving for their children's college fund. Mr. Crawford seemed puzzled and sometime later, returned with a velvet feinting couch and parlor chairs which delighted Eva. Her joy about this good fortune, upon William's arrival home, was promptly snuffed. He angrily questioned her lack of faith in him to be the provider of his home. He sulked off, with Eva still defending her domestic lode.

Months later, a bouncing baby girl, was born. She had already shown signs of determination, just as her mother had spoken over her. She grabbed noses and fingers, and moved from place to place with ease. She would curl her fingers away from the piano, to William's delight, and he would call her daddy's boy, from time to time. They named her Moira, and she would learn all the business lessons her daddy could teach in one lifetime. She wore a watch before any of the children she knew, and soon learned that time was money, and she had none of either to waste. She started a bug collecting business, where she earned a quarter for every bug she picked from obliging gardeners. Soon she had mounted the family horse, and collected mail for family and neighbors, or ran other errands as needed.

William grew confident in his offspring and entertained the idea of a son who could take his place one day. He was sure the banking business was no place for a woman. Moira inadvertently encouraged those thoughts by complaining that all her schoolmates had company at home. It was later determined that company meant, siblings, and William would not deprive her from many things, including people, if she really needed them. He would do his duty, and fulfill his latent wish, also. Eva seemed as if she had become despondent towards William, but he would never be denied by her, or any female for that matter. Eva spited him for taking her for granted that night, and told him so. He reminded her that there were many a good women who envied her position right now, and she should be thankful for this good fortune. She only sighed at the thought of not having given them the chance of knowing such envy and fortune.

Another male, born on time, and lifeless brought an unsettling calm to the house. Awaiting neighbors hung their heads and consoled Eva before departing. Alone with William, he cast suspicious eyes towards her, but said nothing. She would not allow him to abandon her this time. Mr. Crawford appeared, and began packing Eva's belongings. Moira also found herself in her granddaddy's car headed for his home. William was left alone, with his anger that night. And Eva found herself in the comfort of her daddy's arms, but she was no longer his little girl. William had seen to that. She had become a woman by his hand. She cried for both of them—all of them.

Several months passed when William had come full circle with Eva, spying her leaving the store. Once more he eyed her, but it was with more determination than ever, to win her back that he devised a plan to "bump into her." Walking around the block and up the side alley, he casually brushed her shoulder, with amazing timing. She pretended surprise, and exchanged cordialities with him. Had she known the town rodeo was underway, and could he take Moira? Eva knew how desperately Moira needed to see her daddy and so arranged for the visit.

Moira had waited all morning by the parlor window for her daddy's visit. She squealed with delight upon seeing his gleaming Packard roll up the drive. Running through the gate, which gave way to her fanciful flight, she jumped to his waiting arms. Eva carefully approached William, and spoke to him from the gate entrance. She too, had errands to run and would make it easy on them by picking Moira up at his house. Eva enjoyed having some time to herself. It had been some time since she had the pleasure of her own thoughts, without some interruption. She found the ladies of her social club anxious to share time with her, and became lost in the gossip. It was late when she realized that Moira would need to be picked up from William's house. She panicked at what he must be thinking about her maternal abilities. She ran up to the house and almost stumbled into Williams arms. She began explaining and apologizing in earnest, when she noticed William half smirking at her exhausted face. Was he laughing at her on top of all the valiant efforts she had made to get there. Was he mocking her once again, because she had just proven his exacting expectations of incompetence about her? Just as her expression changed to one of anger, he gently covered her lips. It was fine to have extra time to herself. Mr. Crawford had picked up Moira some time ago, and she was probably home in bed by now. Giving a sigh of relief, she half swung at him with her purse for such a teasing and tumbled to the lawn, taking him with her tangled purse. They found themselves laughing at their folly, when Eva caught herself and began straightening her demeanor. The small rose arbor tumbled on them, and once again they laughed among the roses. Suddenly

William yelped in pain, upon realizing one of the thorns had found him. They deftfully maneuvered their way out from the spiked garland, as Eva began nursing his finger back to health. He had never appreciated her tender touch as much as he did now. Her absence had made him grow fonder of her. She feigned scorn at his advances and continued her nursing duties. Caught up in healing kisses, he transcended her misgivings and patiently caressed her deep longings for him. Considering her captured, he locked her in his embrace and enthralled her with considerable effort and reward through the night.

Eva awoke to breakfast in bed. William had decided he would win Eva back, and he spared none of his resources. Eva felt that his intentions were sincere. She walked through the house and longed to be a part of it, once more. When she caught William gazing at her in the entrance, she swooned before him and fell to the feinting couch. He told her that she could only be awakened by the kiss of a prince. He knelt before her, kissed her, and met her gazing eyes with his. Now, he instructed, she must come to his castle, where she would be made his queen. She followed him back to their room, where time once more stood still.

The phone rang, stirring them from their dreams. It was Mr. Crawford wondering how the estranged couple was getting along. He had always figured that some time alone together might help to patch things up. Eva told him it was time for Moira to come home. And once again the family found themselves reunited.

Eva found that it did not take much time to return to the routine of caring for her home. She had also taken in several students for piano lessons, and music helped to fill the once broken places in her home. She had also been selected secretary of the ladies social club, and found herself busy with its activities. As days went by, she found herself desperately seeking out her monthly issue. She could not bare the thought of going through another miscarriage with William. He seemed resigned to his bank duties now, and they were in established routines now. This could surely bring about unsettled emotions from both of them. Her monthly search was in vain, though. She was with child, and she fought back that fount of tears that would only seek to drown her. She would wait as long as possible before she would share her secret with William. That would be best.

William knew his wife very well and sensed her nervousness. He also knew all too well what this usually meant, but he too, pretended all was well, and went about his duties. It was only when Eva fell on the stairs, that she gave away her secret. She clutched her front, and cried for her baby's protection. William heard and came to her side. He rested his head on Eva's breast and held her for some time. Ambiguities filled his head of all the devastating possibilities to come—but with several miscarriages behind her, Eva knew this feeling all too well and comforted and stroked him gently until his fear had somewhat subsided. Until the day of delivery, this could possibly be the last time he would trust her warm bosom as a place of solace. Misgivings began to swell within her, also. She had been given several chances at motherhood, but William and Moira were the only proof that she had vaguely succeeded at it. She felt her fetal losses only as failures against her, and never healed from them. But this time would be different. She recalled the resolve she had found during Moira's pregnancy. For the sake of the life within her, she could not allow herself to fall into the dismal place of self-blame and haunting she knew all too well. She was maturing for all of them now, and was ascending to the place of maternal sacrifice with relative ease. Her reassuring squeeze seemed to surprise William, and her new found strength caused disillusionment about her dependency on him. The melding moment was broken, as he abruptly left her outstretched arms, and headed for the door to work, mumbling about some unfinished business. She arose, and before dutifully attending to the day's chores, delayed them with a piano song to herself-Ode to Joy, played with much fortissimo.

On a fair day as any, Pauline Grace was born to William and Eva. She was as lovely as the day she was birthed on, everyone seemed to agree. William's disappointment from the lack of a male namesake was temporarily overshadowed by the beautiful baby girl that belonged to him. He held the child a slight distance from his body, and stared at her for some time. He glimpsed within, her mother's captivating charms, and established a venerate bond for what he then resolved was his final attempt at establishing respectable lineage. Moira sensed a disruption in the pecking order and promptly grabbed at Williams coattails for some understanding. She received a perfunctory hug and was gently patted on her way. Eva, and Granddad Crawford filled the gap somewhat, but Moira found herself constantly defending her social order.

Eva found that her girls were bringing her more joy than she had ever known she possessed. She poured her college training into every part of the girls she could. Her mother's social graces, learned from years of domestic duty on wealthy plantations, placed them at a distinct advantage from many of the town folk. William, too, enjoyed the lavish praise given to his elegant family, and would take regular Sunday drives into town to show them, and his latest model car, off to the admiring and jealous, alike. Eva noticed that William enjoyed the place of respect he had found in Boley, but realized that her father was providing more and more of her family's upkeep. William considered many of her purchases frivolous, and demanded that she curtail her spending to necessities only. He alone, would determine if a purchase was needed. Eva became more frustrated with her need to constantly call on her parents for her purchases. She found a teaching position in nearby Muskogee county, and waited for the dust to settle upon informing William. It never did. Instead, she found herself reeling from his insults toward her, and his accusations that she doubted his abilities to be the man of the house. She assured him that Moira and Pauline were fine staying with their grandparents while she worked. Moira chimed in, in defense of her mother, and William's seething disappointment at their apparent siding against him manifested. He whipped her soundly, and she ran sobbing to her sister's arms. Eva found herself defenseless against his rantings, and threatened to leave. The next morning found the children searching for their mother, and William looking for a way to save face.

The hunter had become the prey as Eva had managed to plumb the depths of William's frustrations. Deep down, he knew the real enemies of his peace were still to be confronted. If Eva could summon the courage for independence, he could, too. She would not defeat him in that most important facet of social constructions; keeping face. Before the girls could sense the depths of the family's dissolution, William announced a family vacation to his hometown down south, sans mother.

It was Moira's and Pauline's first visit to the deep south and away from the safe confines of their town, Boley. They found themselves both sullen and excited at the thought of leaving mother behind and traveling to their father's birthplace. They watched the familiar Oklahoma scenery leave them far behind as they traveled the dusty roads south. William had struggled often with the desire to return to his birthplace. This visit, he hoped, would free him from the many thoughts he had kept alive about being a slave to his past. He hoped his new found independence and freedom in Boley had unshackled him from this past. He would have to find out by going back to his beginnings.

William daydreamed about what the old homestead would look like now. It had been many years since he struck out on his own, with some bad blood left among them. But he knew that he was always welcome home, and was not disappointed as he pulled up the long drive to the place called home. He had not sent news of his arrival, and surprised his folks with his visit and their grandchildren besides! His dad gave him a hearty hug and kissed his neck. Momma swooped up the girls and led them to the welcoming kitchen were lemonade was waiting. It was rare to find any place that accommodated colored folks traveling on distant road trips and they had driven the many miles with a few gas stops only. The lemonade was the girls reminder that they had done a good job of "holding their water" and needed a bathroom in the worst way. They had never used an outside bathroom before, and were rescued after some time had elapsed while they searched for the pull chain. Grandma called them sophisticated city folk, and smiled at all the wonderful news regarding her son's fortune. It was not all good news, William thought, but he did not want to spoil the reunion time they were sharing. He could stay a few days, but had quite a bit of work to attend to upon his return. His brother, Eli was working at the town gas station and would be home soon. William said the car needed a fill up and drove down to meet his estranged brother. The family had kept some things unknown to William, also. His brother walked to the rear of the car without acknowledging William's presence, at all. William asked for a fill up and got out of the car to see his brother. Eli's hands trembled slightly as he pumped the gas, and his eyes were swollen and "sleep" filled. He squinted at William, before realizing he was gazing at his own brother. William sensed a sadness about him, along with a whiff of spirits, but slowly extended his hand towards him. Eli passed on the shake and embraced his long gone brother. He would see him back home and there they would catch up on their missed past—an idea that came none too soon, as Eli was quickly reminded by his boss to get back to work if he wanted his job. William returned to his car and headed back. He would take his girls to visit their "other" grandfather, a visit he dreaded, more than any, to make.

It had not been relayed to William about Boss Ed's dire health condition. William had come at the time he was on his death bed. Eternal servants at the great house were found in various degrees of mourning. Some were found smiling and cajoling near the back entrance, waiting for the death knell that would end their misery. Others, more dread full, were weeping near the bedroom entrance when William arrived. He hesitated often, and even turned to exit from a side entrance, then turned around once again and walked to the bedroom chamber. Two young colored girls were lightly alternating the pulling of a rope attached to palm fans on the ceiling. Pauline found it difficult to discern if she was holding her daddy's hand or if he was holding hers. She did not understand his uneasiness at seeing her grandfather, until white netting was pulled to one side, and there confronting her was a large white, ghost of a man, bellowing a greeting to them. He found William's success stories entertaining, and laughed himself into a coughing fit, accompanied with backslapping hacking. It was the closest Pauline had ever been to death, but Moira showed the repose of a veteran. He inquired about our admittance, and pretentiously smiled when he discovered the back entrance had not been used. William was overwhelmed by Boss Ed's debilitating weakness. He would have, in the past, played one of his parlor games on William and directed them to the back door to try again, but that was now part of his past. He would not summon the strength to humiliate anyone again. He was conserving all efforts to delay his last gasp of life.

Boss Ed's son entered and motioned for William to follow him into the adjacent room. He stopped short of accusing William of being a gravedigger of his father's inheritance and asked William how much it would take to make him "go away." Unwittingly he had empowered a man who moments ago, had felt powerless in the foreboding place of his beginnings. He would get back with him some time later was all that William could manage to say. It was time for his children to be tended to.

The news of William reaping inheritance benefits from an old plantation master sent chills through his parents. They knew that some of the town's good old boys would do their best to make Boss Ed's son the sole heir by seeing to it that William disappeared—permanently. He should leave as soon as possible. William was a soldier and didn't approve of the idea of running. He had faced some of the stiffest military opposition Europe had to offer, and survived. Still, he had his daughters to think about. He would have his attorney in Boley write up the necessary paperwork to claim his unexpected inheritance and have it sent to Boss Ed's son, post haste. A preliminary investigation by William's attorney of Boss Ed's estate value revealed its worth as somewhere over several million dollars!

It was dusk when William departed from his old haunting grounds. He wondered if he'd ever return to the humble old log cabin again. A car, approaching head on, jarred him from his musings as he jerked the wheel and avoided being side swiped. The girls were tousled, but unharmed. The car engine idled, and William waited for the engine to turn over, wondering if the fleeing driver had "accidentally" meant them harm. An officer arrived at the scene and marched up to William's car. He asked him what business he had with that 'nigga child' in the back seat. He poked his churlish face farther into the car and flashed his light in the girl's faces. He acknowledged that Pauline must be his, on second thought, and sent them on their way.

The outside world seemed strange and forbidding that year they visited the south. It would seem like forever, before they could breathe a sigh of relief, to be back in beloved Boley, again.

Chapter 5--The Times are a Changing

The weary travelers made their way to the Oklahoma state line just after daybreak. William had traveled all night to make his way out of the sweltering, oppressive south. He had not received any news regarding Eva's whereabouts, and headed to Mr. Crawford's home. They had heard the engine approaching up the driveway and were a sight for the sore tired eyes of William and the children. Mrs. Crawford ushered them off to familiar sleeping quarters, and they rested wistfully until noon. They were awakened by the wonderful aroma of Mrs. Crawford's baked ham and beans. They gratefully acknowledged their appreciation of her efforts by consuming every bit of the delicious meal. Stuffed and happy, they managed a dessert of her delectable peach cobbler with a glass of cold milk. The meal proved to be a temporary distraction as the girls soon busied themselves inquiring about their mother's whereabouts. William told them they would see her sometime later, but for now, it was time to comb Granddad's hair. William set about searching for Eva's whereabouts while Moira and Pauline began their vacation dispatches with Granddad Crawford. He departed under the chuckles of Mr. Crawford who had heard Moira's description of the log cabin her daddy lived in just like Abraham Lincoln.

His girls had given him a sense of urgency in the search for Eva. He did not have quite the nurturing spirit she possessed and did not know how to calm the fear he saw in their eyes. He drove home in earnest, hoping she had left some indication of her plans there. When he pulled up to the house, there were no signs of life present. It was eerily vacant when he entered, even the lingering smells of family life absent. Eva had been away for some time he figured. He surveyed their bedroom and located a small white note card on her dressing table. It was filled with news about her new teaching job, one that would take her to many parts of the state, and how good it was to have the ability to make her own financial decisions. He became more enraged with every line he read, and tossed the note aside. With slight deliberation, he called his attorney and began proceedings to divorce Eva.

He quietly drove back to Mr. Crawford's, not sure about how he could begin such a weighty conversation with a man who had been so generous towards him.

Pauline was sobbing in Grandma's arms on the front porch when he arrived. Grandma consoled, and Grandad scolded. He asked William where in thunder these kids got the idea they were white folks and what was he going to do about it. William explained about their meeting with Boss Ed, down south, which may have caused some of the confusion. Pauline interrupted however, and enlightened them all by sharing that Grandma Crawford said she was white, too. And everybody was confusing her, so she must be both colored and white.

Mr. Crawford looked askance at his wife and continued, "You girls are old enough to know by now that we live with laws, not all of them are just but they are the rules we are living by, just the same. Now, in this state called Oklahoma, if you have one drop of colored blood in you, you are by law a colored person. Here in Boley, we can be proud of that distinction, and show any man that God is no respecter of persons, with the honor and diligent labors we bring to our race."

Moira gently interrupted and reminded her grandfather that they didn't really live in Boley, because they weren't wanted there neither.

Grandma smiled triumphantly, "And a child shall lead them."

"And where in the Scripture does it say you can change your stripes?" Granddad Crawford countered.

"You'd better bury me as a white citizen," Grandma Crawford demanded, "or I'll come back and haunt you with a vengeance, Clint Crawford."

"Not if I go before you," he chuckled to himself.

Grandma Crawford sat back in her rocker sulking. William sensed this was not the time to add the burden of another dissolution with them. It took some time for everyone to repose and continue with business as usual.

William gathered the girls and led them to the car. They waved goodbye to their Grandparents and headed home. A light from the front window told them that someone was inside. The girls rushed to the door and demanded its opening. They squealed upon seeing their mothers smiling face welcoming them with open arms. They had so much to tell her and barely breathed between stories. They felt as if they had been bottled up inside. Mother called them, "hot-house flowers." William barely managed a greeting before sending the girls to their rooms. He and mother had private words to discuss—they would have to continue sharing with their mother, later. Mother had two presents waiting for them, which downplayed their disappointment of unfinished "girl talk." They obediently went to their rooms, barely closing the door when William began his tirade. How dare she leave him with the children, without telling him. How dare she find employment without telling him. How dare she... Eva interrupted his rantings with newfound courage obtained from being on her own. How much charity did he expect from her parents? It had become downright embarrassing, and she was not going to put up with it any more. William mounted with his final coup, as he informed her that he would not be putting up with her ramblings anymore. He then added insult to injury by telling her she was unfit to rear any namesake of his, which must explain her inability to bear him a son. No sooner than the words left his mouth he knew he had touched a sore spot with her, and she immediately left the room sobbing. He knew he had gone too far to turn back now. She needed consoling more than he, but he didn't have enough strength for the both of them. Moira and Pauline had heard too, and were hurting. Neither of their parents realized the need the girls had for consoling, but the girls cried for all the family's pain that night.

Somber faces greeted the new day and the breakfast table was lacking the familiar conversations of daily plans. The girls headed off to school, not knowing if mother would be there when they arrived back. The school day proved long and dreary, and Pauline could hardly wait to find Moira at her usual pickup spot for the walk home. Daddy asked if chores had been started when he arrived home that evening. He called Moira and Pauline his boys, when work had been satisfactorily completed in the garden. It wasn't long before Granddad Crawford, too, would tease the girls about being his boys. The only exception to this was when he teased that he would give a quarter if a promise was kept not to cut off their long braids. Quite a bit of pocket change was made by the girls from this game.

One particular evening William arrived home melancholy, and asked about his boys. Mother scolded him for such a reference and emphatically stated that she would have no tomboys around her home. This only seemed to delight him, her dislike of his pleasures, and he continued all the more. Mother told him that it was apparent that he would take no delight in pleasing her, and she found a few pleasures of her own in town today. William's curiosity was piqued by her innuendo, when she disappeared in the bedroom and returned with a stunning moiré evening dress. It would have to go back he insisted, he would refuse payment for it. She now retaliated with the fact that she had purchased the dress with her own money. Moira chimed in with comments about mother needing to feel pretty, when William turned and whacked her for what he called impudent behavior. Momma rose to comfort her, but William turned her away. Momma threatened she would leave if he hurt them again, but it all became too much for Pauline. She ran for the cooling shade of a meadow tree for comfort. Her beautiful family was coming apart—how could such a thing happen?

Dinner had been delayed too long, and the Kalamazoo stove sent a spark through the kitchen that quickly ignited the floor and adjoining brooder house. Neighbors united and brought the fire under control. Mother said this surely was a sign of more no good things to come.

Perhaps she had spoken her fate into existence, perhaps she was only prophesizing, no matter, she would see her words come to pass. William began accusing her of attempting to destroy his house. He began finding fault in many of her routine activities. Burdened beyond measure, and with her emotional and physical health deteriorating, she arranged to leave and visit distant relatives. She drove to her father's house who unknowingly began assisting her in a flight from her pain. Of course William knew she was leaving, he encouraged her to go—which actually was not very far from the truth. She had tried to hide from her father how estranged she and William had become, but daddies always sense when daughters are in trouble. She would not confide in him completely, and he sent her off, bewildered about her state of affairs.

A late call from William confirmed his fears. He was sure that Eva had left him, and he needed to do what any man would do. Mr. Crawford was caught in the middle and wanted to make things better for all of them, for he too, had a stake in their success. He had placed his name on the line for William, including one that would secure him on the bank board and the Lodge. William's desperate tones told him that his mind had been made up. He had some unfinished business to settle, and would need their help assisting with the girls.

The following day William went to his attorney with his petition for divorce. He would be filing abandonment charges, along with emotional instability, against Eva. The news quickly spread through the small town of Boley. Several of Eva's lodge members sought her out to begin their dalliances with her response. She hastily returned from her visiting retreat and found herself in a whirlwind of self-defense. Stares and telephone intrusions were constant. She thought it would be best if the town did not have her around to gossip about, and made plans to leave.

The ladies from her lodge, however, were not about to watch their fellow member leave without a fight. A late meeting one night helped to bolster Eva. The ladies had gathered full circle, and decided that Eva had been mistreated and appropriate steps would be taken for her protection.

Quite a bit of bargaining was going on over Eva. She was prayed over, chanted over. One of the members offered her an infallible "roots" recipe, guaranteed to make him crawl back to her. They decided that old William had mistreated a fellow member and he would get what was coming to him. The ladies consoled Eva and assured her that she would always have a friend in them. She suspected that a few of the ladies weren't altogether altruistic about their distaste for William, especially when they asked for his phone number so they could call and let him know just how they felt. But she left the meeting buoyed by the strength and support she had been given that night. She hummed to herself quietly. It had been some time since she had a song in her heart.

Sunday morning found Grandma Crawford walking from church with her own inspirational song. "For thou O Lord art a shield for me..." She shared with Eva pastor's message: "Somebody's going to need the Lord's divine protection around here. Are you keeping faith, honey?" Eva shared that she had the blessed assurance from her lodge friends about what she needed to do and that her faith led her to believe that William would surely get what he deserved for all the hurt he had caused her. Mrs. Crawford sensed her daughter's bitterness, and reminded her that vengeance could only come from the Lord, and He most assuredly didn't need any help from the likes of some of those minxes. And, she gently reminded Eva if she had forgotten that some of them showed up at her wedding upset about not being the bride themselves. Eva insisted those feelings came about due to the stress of the occasion, and her friends were solidly behind her. Raised on Scripture, she shared her thoughts about a mother bear robbed of her welts, and reminded her mother that her children had been taken from her.

Mrs. Crawford played peacemaker, called the girls to her side, and counseled, "These girls are with us much of the time, and you know this is by William's design." She gently shooed them off and continued. "He says you haven't been yourself lately anyway, always talking about being depressed and ..."

Eva interrupted, "Momma you can't be sidin' with him, too! That's how he took my babies from me, telling everybody lies about my abilities. I simply refused to be his child, Momma, that's all. I'm a full grown woman, now, and I will not be denied who I was meant to be. Going out to work was the best thing I could have done. I should be glad to be rid of him."

Mother was not dissuaded. Gently she counseled Eva about the conversations they had about the thirteen years between her and William and how difficult it had been convincing her that she was not as grown as she thought. She stressed, "Even your chaperoning brother's presence couldn't discourage you two. You were bound and determined to marry the man, Eva, and there was something there between you two."

Eva defended her decision with confessions of how much William had changed on her—that's what makes marriage a mystery and a fear, wasn't it? Eva interjected, "How can anyone know such a thing? How could I know he would blame me for losing his son? Accusing me of not taking proper care of myself. Said I was 'too blue—that's why I was having all them blue babies,' he said. Just mean, spiteful things. I was hurting too, and I needed him to care. He was just as blue as I was. Why didn't he care? I just needed him to care, was all..." she began weeping.

Mother wrapped her daughter's head in her arms and hushed her down. Pastor was right, she thought. We all in need of the Lord's divine protection.

The girls had learned to make the best of their family's unfortunate circumstances. Grandma Crawford taught them how to can vegetables, sew, and assist the farmhands with the fruit they helped pick from the orchard. Busy hands kept away any idle hearts or minds. Summer was coming to and end also, which meant preparation time for the harsh winters that swept across the plains. Fruits and vegetables were coming in by the bushels to the Crawford kitchen, when the low humming sound of a plane engine was heard. The girls ran excitedly to the meadow with Granddad Crawford trailing behind, admonishing them to stay clear of the landing field. Several of the field hands were pointing toward the clear blue sky at the single engine prop plane circling for a landing. It swooped down, aligned itself between the worn dirt tracks in the meadow, and glided in for a smooth landing. The single blades whirred briskly and then choked to a halt. Planes were still a novel proposition to most folks, and they always meant important news was forthcoming. Granddad Crawford, along with some of the field men, rushed to meet the pilot, a Mr. Wiley Post, whose face seemed full of worry. He jumped from the plane and began moving his arms wildly, as he explained to Mr. Crawford the news. It was big news from nearby Wewoka county. Their bank had been robbed for the second time in a month. The town had been put in dire straits to make payments due. He had come to warn Mr. Crawford and the Boley bank board about tightening up security around their bank. It appeared the job was done by Pretty Boy Floyd's gang, he conjectured. "Darnedest thing, though," he added, "they seem to disappear into the countryside every time we get them on the run. Seems as if most of Cooksom Hills is cheering him on and protecting him. We're bumfuzzled as can be, but determined to catch those thieves. There's a lot of talk going around that Floyd's sending scouts into your town. Hope you all don't have to take them scoundrels on." Mr. Crawford informed the pilot that Boley didn't take kindly to thieves and gunslingers, and Floyd and his boys would find that out lightnin' quick. The pilot saluted him on and went on his way.

It was difficult for Moira and Pauline to see their Granddad talking so seriously. They had rarely seen him in such an agitated state as he was now. He went on his way to tell the other men of the town the big news. It would be a late meeting, by the time he gathered all the men and discussed a plan of action. He asked that dinner be saved for him and that extra protection would be needed around here. Grandma had already heard the news from pastor on Sunday, "somebody's going to need the Lord's divine protection."

Boley men everywhere heard the cry to arms and prepared to meet at the Masonic Temple to discuss a plan for protecting the town. The Mayor, J.D. Turner, opened the emergency meeting by informing the men about several recent bank robberies in the county. He told the men that it had been known for some time that Floyd and his boys had been eyeing the town in an attempt to rob its bank. He rallied the men with his booming voice, about how much more was at stake then stolen cash, a robbery would impact the town in the worst way, business lost, homes foreclosed—it could mean the very survival of the town. It was a challenge they would meet head on—"Remember Poison Springs," he thundered! Soon hearty applause could be heard from the street, as the men roused themselves—"Men," he continued, "at Poison Springs we fought our enemy head on, and knew his tactics, but this is a new breed of enemy, he moves like a cat, and makes no rebel yell to give warning. Men, I'm not so sure we've prepared ourselves for this kind of threat." Loud outcries of disagreement followed, "I'll take any gunslinger on!" "Here's a quiet riter for them Floyd boys!" "Bring em on!" the men yelled. When things settled down a bit, old Mr. Johnson spoke up. "Didn't you all here what the gent said. They're coming without warning. How are you going to prepare for them, when they don't plan to tell you when they'll get here?" It was just the question for which Mr. Jones was waiting. He had come from Tuskeegee's Institute and brought with him some ideas that had been used up north. He claimed they had all kinds of newfangled devices that could be used to protect the bank. One of the men teasingly called out—"You mean a trap door?" which caused the men to howl with laughter. Mr. Jones didn't mind the derision, though—he had something more sophisticated than that in mind. But without the element of surprise, the device was useless. He simply asked them to have their guns ready if they ever heard the bank alarm ring through the town. The mayor continued with words of keeping gun supplies stocked and… just as he was about to finish, young Lank Henson appeared through the large wooden doors. Somewhat breathless, he began sharing that one of Floyd's boys was over at the Hamburger Shoppe buying sundaes for the folks! "Bet he's scoutin' the place too," Henson added.

Several of the men, fired up from the discussion, went for the door, when the mayor interrupted. "Buying sundae's never been a crime in Oklahoma—besides, Slim could use the business, too. We'll keep an eye on him, let him spend all the money he can in our fair town. He probably thinks he's going to get it back—we'll see about that, won't we fellas?" A rousing cheer of approval went up. The mayor asked that no one get out of line, and that the town continue in their usual pursuits unless things dictated otherwise. With that he admonished the men to get back to the business of keeping the town running, and bid them a good evening.

Mr. Crawford began his trek home when William alighted beside him. "How about that," he started, "Boley a target for the big boys!" Mr. Crawford admonished William about getting too fired up about events by reminding him that "those big boys" had been using machine guns to conduct their business. William was undaunted, and quipped about the Germans doing the same thing, and how they had managed to get them all settled down. "They *managed* quite a bit of damage in the process, though, didn't they?" Mr. Crawford chided. William guessed from Mr. Crawford's tone that things were more serious than he had imagined. His wife's words about folks needing the Lord's protection was cause for pause for both of them. They both knew that prophesied warnings brought the dual meaning of the need for supernatural intervention along with the force of Hades. There was a sure enough storm brewing, and native folks knew that meant real trouble in the land of rip snortin' tornadoes. William continued stirring things up when he asked Mr.

Crawford if he had been thinking the worst about him since his divorce proceedings from Eva. He had hoped that Mr. Crawford understood that he had never meant to... Mr. Crawford quickly interrupted William upon hearing his daughter mentioned so casually. He told him that "not meaning and then doing," is no match made in heaven. "We're family bound folks, William. You struggle with that don't you, son?"

William unburdened himself before Mr. Crawford by telling him how difficult it had been growing up his whole life with folks making him wonder where he belonged. It was true, though, family was not a concept that he had embraced or with which he was even comfortable. Mr. Crawford had him pegged right about that. But he did not have any idea how his daughter, too, had struggled with her identity, and how difficult it was to help her find her true worth to him just as she was. He was certain she never allowed him to love her fully. She was holding back on him, while he had given her everything a woman could want. Mr. Crawford listened, having heard and seen the vast disparities between their stories. One thing he did share with William was his knowledge that not one goes through life without trials and difficulties, and his own cross to bear. The only thing that mattered was how you held out and how you finished. He told William there was a whole lot of good in the world, and that Boley was a part of it—showing the world that race doesn't matter and you're only as disadvantaged as you want to be—everywhere, everyday people prospering and making do with the God-given talents they have the freedom to use here in Boley. "Stay with it," Mr. Crawford insisted, and then rode off.

William had come to miss his fledgling family, but his talk with Mr. Crawford confirmed what he already knew—too much had happened between him and Eva to ever bring things back to the way they needed to be. He would resolve himself to bachelorhood once again. There would always be a place for Eva in his heart, but he would make sure that he never plumbed the depths of love so deeply again. He found his solitary life less of a struggle than he had anticipated, as there was no dearth of beautiful women in Boley. One, in particular, had decided that William's solitary days were over, and made advances his way. She proved difficult to miss with all her beauty. For William, she was the compulsory "years younger" than he. Perhaps she was ready to listen and obey his every command and allow him to be the man in charge. She was actually from nearby Grayson, a town also known as Wild Cat. It was a name that proved to be an ominous portent of things to come.

William found she possessed all the domestic skills required for duty. She was slight in appearance and only nineteen years old. She became Moira and Pauline's "Little Mother." Once again, William found favor with Mr. Crawford and the trustees at Farmers and Merchants Bank and purchased his second homestead of ten acres several miles from Boley. He would try again, to establish the home life he so desperately desired.

Eva, too, had learned to embrace her new found freedom from miscarriages and malcontent. She was traveling around Muskogee teaching and finishing her studies at Langston College in the summer. She returned to Boley one evening and began catching up on correspondences sent in her absence. One in particular kept her attention for some time. It was from her brother, and described William's new happy family. Visibly shaken, she dropped to the chaise, and continued reading. After holding the letter to her bosom for some time, she released it and concluded she was due for some happiness too. What, she reasoned, was stopping her? Certainly not William's distant taunts. Yes, she thought, there was still enough love to go around for her, too. Not long after discarding the missive, she began the search for her own personal happiness, this time on her own terms.

Chapter 6--A Shield for Me

William's new-found happiness proved to be short-lived. There was more than a baby in this cradle that he had robbed—and baby could she tussle! This Helen, her trousseau removed, revealed a tough, resilient young lady who loathed being told what to do. He had been warned that she was from the nearby town called Wild Cat. And he soon regretted that he had not better inquired about its residents. Warnings from others about falling *for* love too soon fell on deaf ears. Once again, William and Oklahoma found themselves sharing in the throes of most of the nation's discord.

Robbing and starving had reached a fever pitch by the 1930's. Too many folks had become frustrated with the state of affairs and some had decided to take matters into their own hands. Bank robberies were occurring with increased frequency, especially in Oklahoma. Boley townspeople were on edge, even though the town still remained untouched from the rash of recent robberies. It proved unsettling all the more, when yet another robbery was reported in neighboring Earlsboro. Would Floyd and his boys succeed in dismantling a whole town, by disrupting the business of its only bank? When would he be stopped before more were hurt?

These anxious summer days were waning, and hope was fading for an end to the anguish caused by violence and desperation. Cooler days replaced summer's stifling pace. Skifts lightly covered Indian Blankets, whose blooms had faded some time ago. It was the belief held by the Kiowa natives that these flowers symbolized good luck—contrarily, the scarlet markings on the petals of those remaining bore silent witness to the bloodshed to come.

It was colored bandit Pete Glass who had decided on the calculated risk to use autumn as the right time to rob a Negro bank. He figured the coolin' off time would have most folks off guard and unsuspecting of a holiday "hit." He arranged a meeting with Charles "Pretty Boy" Floyd and his tall lieutenant, Birdwell, to instruct them on how to "rob a colored" bank. He felt his Negro descent gave him alone this privileged perch, but was soon dismissed by Floyd and told that Boley was still too risky a town. Floyd instead, headed for Earlsboro, where he would prove to his boys that he was not "soft on niggers" as rumor had it. Pete Glass meanwhile would remain close to Boley, preparing to prove his point. He had secretly convinced Birdwell that it was time for him to go solo, and prove that part of his Cherokee, along with his Irish, manhood. CW Patterson, of Kiowa descent, would round off the bandit pack.

Up in Earlsboro Floyd had once again provided fodder for the newsboys. The town's police chief had recently confiscated Floyd's car. Floyd forced a Negro, employed in the police chief's service, to open his door, whereupon he found himself in Floyd's discharge. The Negro was used as a shield to gain access to Floyd's car. Floyd discharged and emptied the gun, and handed it back to the chief. He promptly fled the scene, after making an open show of law and order. Newspapers faithfully dispatched every detail of the brazen criminal act, to Floyd's glee and law enforcement's chagrin. That, Floyd thought, would show them who was "soft on niggers." His ride back through the Cooksom Hills of Oklahoma was filled with the imaginations of storytelling with which he would fill the heads of his faithful sidekicks.

However, Floyd had not familiarized himself with the verse that taught "no honor among thieves." His sidekicks were no longer faithfully awaiting his arrival. They were preparing to become legends in their own mind. They had spent the night at Pete Glass sister's house near Earlsboro, and had been given breakfast by colored farmer Doc Bearns. They had spent several days beforehand in the pool hall across the street from the Boley bank scouting out escape routes. They had done everything they could to prepare themselves for that fateful ride into its town and history.

It was Thanksgiving eve, November 1932, and station KVOO announced the coldest temperature on record for that date. The bitter cold had, for the most part, emptied the streets. Still, some folks were shopping for Thanksgiving extras, in addition to gun shells, for the next day's quail hunting season. Most of the townspeople conserved their energy for banter about who would win the high school basketball game between the Boley Bears and the Wewoka Lions.

During the ride into Boley, Birdwell continued reading Bible verses aloud. This tradition he had begun with Floyd, he superstitiously thought, might bring them the same luck on this, his first solo heist. The combination, however, was no match made in heaven, and there was no way for him to know that luck was finally running out for most big-name robbers of this era. He completed a verse from Psalms and remained silent until the brown sedan slowly rolled into town. This bandit trio, Glass, Patterson, and Birdwell slid from their car seats, set well-polished shoes and boots on the town's dirt street and were instantly spotted as sticking out like "whores at a church picnic." It was half past ten in the quiet town of Boley, when bandits Patterson and Birdwell slinked into the heart of the town—Farmers and Merchants Bank. Patterson had concealed his weapon under his overcoat, and Birdwell's weapon of choice, his colt 45 revolver was packed by his side. Pete Glass had decided he would serve best as the outside lookout and stealthily strode across the main street.

William found himself in a sullen mood that fateful morning, as he had fitfully dealt with Helen regarding his half prepared breakfast. He had managed to suit up, however, for the upcoming Thanksgiving holiday, and buffed down to his spectators for the occasion. His mind on Helen, he barely took note of the tall stranger's brusque entrance to his cage. William's demand for him to produce identification only caused the fellow more agitation, which hastened employee Mack McCormick's slip into the bank's steel vault for his shotgun. His suspicions about a possible robbery were on target. Birdwell's booming voice yelled the intent of a holdup! William had rarely practiced for this moment, as he had allowed himself to believe, albeit half-heartedly, in Boley's sacredness. His military prowess instinctively took over, and he moved as he was ordered from the safe confines of his cage by the end of a sawed off shotgun now pointed in his side. It was decided by Birdwell that William would be his hostage. A second demand by his partner CW Patterson for all the money was interrupted by a resounding alarm. The element of surprise had kicked in. The last dollar pulled had been rigged to sound the alarm. The Tuskegee gent, Mr. Jones, as promised, had set up his secret weapon in the cashier's drawer. The bank's large glass window had provided a stage for gathering curious onlookers. The alarm provided further proof to the anxious crowd that the bank had been assaulted. Bedlam ensued. Mack found a small crack in the bank vault door, and aimed straightway for Birdwell. The shot met its mark, and Birdwell grabbed William as he sputtered forth at Mayor JD Turner. He accused him of pulling the bank's alarm, to which Mayor JD did not back down. He confessed with "damned certainty" that he had, to which Birdwell managed to shoot back, at point blank range, his outrage. The Mayor and Birdwell fell to the floor in unison, at William's feet. Shots broke through the large window, hitting Birdwell's accomplice. Glass ran to the getaway car and found himself facing a volley of shots from the townsfolk who had answered the call to arms. He slumped at the wheel motionless. William was swung to the front entrance of the bank and found himself facing a fusillade of bullets. He was used as a shield by the robber CW Patterson, who found himself with no means of transportation and a mob of angry townsfolk aiming right at him. He pushed William to the side and gave himself up for dead. Suddenly, Lank Henson's wife placed herself between the guns and the outlaw, and pleaded for his life. Folks were in no mood for salvation, and pleaded with her to move from harm's way. She was courageous and unmoved by their hurling threats. Her reputation proved sound, and the angry crowd slowly backed away and allowed justice to have the end of the day. Sometime later, bandit CW Patterson recovered from his wounds and newspaper accounts said before his imprisonment, he graciously went back to thank the "nigger woman" for saving his life.

On that eventful day, however, news of the ill-fated robbery swiftly traveled through the town, right up to the local school. Moira and Pauline had received rumors of the event. They overheard in hushed whispers that the bank had been robbed and all bank employees had been killed by Pretty Boy Floyd and his gang. Pauline's heart sank, but she scarcely believed the news to be true. She thought of her father as invincible, as most schoolgirls do of their daddies. She held on to hope and raced from the school grounds without a care about consequences. As she hurried down roads to the main street, she felt as if she was running an endless marathon. It was the prize of seeing her father's face that drove her weary legs forward. She bounded up to the entrance only to find a wall of spectators blocking her way. She peered through openings in the crowd as her heart raced. Word spread that this was William's daughter, and a child-sized parting was made for her. It was the glint of life from his green eyes that caused Pauline instant relief and joy. She leaped into his arms. He managed to field official's questions and exchange kisses with Pauline. She finally eased her hold on him and noticed his bullet-ridden coattails and the splattered blood that contrasted his white spectator shoes. She remained determinedly attached to him from that day on.

The trauma of the event, along with William's miraculous survival, placed him in surreal time from which most agreed he'd never recover. Becoming a human shield that passed *through* so many bullets far surpassed anything he had ever experienced, even in his military career. But the town's leader and his good friend, JD Turner lay outstretched behind him. He had sacrificed his life for Boley, and had convinced Birdwell that he alone was responsible for sounding the alarm that botched the robbery. William knew this courageous act had probably saved his life. But he knew the town could ill-afford to offer up this sacrificial lamb. When it was discovered that Floyd was not a part of the raid, Boley citizens steeled themselves for perhaps another revenge attack from Floyd.

On Thanksgiving Day, Boley residents found themselves grateful and downhearted. Their bank had survived its first robbery attempt but it came with a high price. The *Boley Progress* that morning quoted William's description of the robbery as "an all out war scene" with him being in the thick of it. Rumor had it, that Birdwell's son Jack, was bound and determined to "tear the damn town apart."

The article continued with a quote from Okfuskee county sheriff "that they would not remove their guard from Boley, and that it was good riddance that Birdwell was gone. But, he continued, he could not be satisfied until Floyd was captured and it would be fine by him if it happened right in Boley." William scoffed at such bravado. He and the town had taken enough and he flatly decided that a gun would grace the door each night. Helen would not hear of such a thing, as it would put the girls in harms way. William countered that his decision was the final word on the subject. Thanksgiving dinner was filled with heated discussions about the food and Floyd, when the phone rang. William had been chosen to be JD Turner's pallbearer, and he was ambivalent in his feelings about the honor. It would be at the funeral, many speculated, where Floyd would exact his revenge for the death of his best comrade, Birdwell. The call produced a welcomed silence to the dinner table, as William mentally prepared himself for the next day's events.

A pall hung over the Negro community, as thousands of mourners made their way by car and sagging wagon into town for the funeral. The procession tramped through the sandy streets and streamed past the large broken bank window that served as the only mute testimony of the melee that had occurred. More than three thousand came to pay homage to the town's bank president and mayor for over ten years. Most could not fit into the small gray home where his body lay in state among banks of floral arrangements and friends. When the time came to carry the casket to the church, William found the building heavily guarded with over fifty plain clothes officers from nearby Tulsa and Okemah. His fleeting glance at Mrs. Turner and JD Turner's five children renewed his courage for the task at hand and he found that it was not long before he could gently lay his friend before his many devotees. JD's eulogy was one of praise for that "rare breed of man who speaks his mind without fear of reprisal." He would always be revered as the man "who gave his life to protect those who trusted him," was the paean most often heard. The reverend also prophesied that the times were in God's hands, and that time was running out for those who found gain in riotous living and robbery. It was clear that folks were in no mood for fear, now, as the courageous actions of the honored dead would be dishonored by such emotions.

Some months went by before the reverend's words proved true. The following year, Charles

"Pretty Boy" Floyd was taken out by law officials in October, giving folks plenty of time to be thankful, and his sympathizers, of which there were not a few, time to mourn. And thus was removed from the nation's Most Wanted List, the "hoodoo hoodlum" Prettyboy Floyd.

Chapter 7--Pulling Up Stakes

William found life in Boley difficult after JD's death. His insight into financial dealings was sorely missed, and William found the town in desperate need of Turner's entrepreneurial abilities. Everywhere, it seemed, things were falling apart. Townsfolk seemed reluctant to make large deposits and investments in the bank now, for leader, JD Turner's domineering presence was no longer their blessed assurance. Adding more discouragement to the situation was the haunting story of what had happened to town hero, Mack McCormick. He had taken Birdwell's gun after the botched robbery attempt and dutifully wore it for what he claimed would be his protection against any further threats against his life. The tables turned on this proud legendary hero when the gun, many believed, avenged its former owner, and accidentally discharged a bullet that became Mack's "thorn in his side." Family members insisted it directly contributed to his early death. Now, William found it increasingly difficult to find himself in the company of trusted friends and confidants.

At home, Helen seemed to grow more and more distant from his advances toward her. Thanks to Mr. Crawford and JD Turner he was well schooled now in discerning opportunity from lack thereof and made plans for new opportunities.

Moira and Pauline had grown into fine young ladies. William no longer worried about their upbringing, as Eva, and the Crawfords, had helped mold them into the well disciplined, aptly social, ingénue. Moira had decided that her place was with her mother Eva, now, and knew she was old enough to take this stand. Pauline could not imagine life without her sister or father, but decided her place was by her father's side. William persevered under these conditions for several years after the bank robbery.

On one particularly trying day, another local business had informed the bank of plans to move elsewhere. It was also discovered that a second bank would come to Boley. Perhaps a new financial face was needed after the nightmare bank robbery attempt. Feeling overwhelmed by all the discouraging news William arrived home to find several new purchases by Helen. It seemed a celebration was in order since Pauline had gained early admission into the same college as Moira. The girls would be united again, as they had desired. William failed to see how this required the need for additional spending on Helen's part, since college tuition could easily be used as celebration enough! Everything would be returned, at his insistence, and she would be placed on a strict budget. Helen fumed and promised him that as soon as the girls left for school, she would follow suit. He made sure all heard him proclaim that a wife was a luxury he would never find use for again.

Sometime later, William found himself in the solitude of his empty home. After sending the girls off to college, Helen had made good on her promise to leave him. He mulled over the letters Pauline had sent him. He was particularly amused by one that told him about how reserved the boys were there. He neglected to tell her that on his initial visit there, one in which the girls found no shortage of male assistance with their belongings, he promised all potential male suitors that they would always be privy to his gun collection. Nevertheless, they were doing well in their studies and enjoying their new-found freedom.

He arose and decided to pay a visit to his loyal friend, Mr. Crawford. As he pulled up to the house, he found bags and luggage being placed in Mr. Crawford's car trunk and his good friend on the way to the city hospital for what he described as a routine visit. William had dealt with death enough times to know there was more to the story than Mr. Crawford had shared. His friend's sullen eyes told more than he could say. He felt the need to apologize to him for never joining his brotherhood of lodge members. Mr. Crawford stopped him short and assured him that surviving the bank robbery had sealed his immortality and need for any expressions of bravado. William insistently assured him that he was no good in the bartering of souls that he had seen so many of the men engaged. Mr. Crawford acknowledged that he may come up short in his bartering this time—which caused William's heart to sink at the innuendo. He watched the car disappear from view and returned home.

He was late with his plan to visit his loyal friend. Mrs. Crawford's voice confirmed what he suspected. Mr. Crawford had passed away. William shared with her that it would no longer be necessary for her to haunt him, as they, at one time, had discussed. She sadly replied that it would be fine if he haunted her for the rest of her days. William knew that this loving couple had demonstrated for him and all who witnessed their devotion, what a true marriage was all about. He sighed deeply with her, offered additional condolences, and bid her goodbye.

William decided that a move farther west was in order and he made inquiries about banking opportunities in California. Mr. Crawford's words about "staying with it" rang hollow with him now. They had made a good run of it, though—maintaining an all-colored town, it just seemed to William that the stakes had become too high. Still, he was encouraged to see young men like himself, with the same optimism he had brought to Boley. Perhaps they would help in the salvation of his town.

Haunting refrains of "Go west, young man," sent him packing and on his solitary way, once again.

Acknowledgments

Grateful acknowledgement is given to my Creator for His boundless Love and inspiration. Also, respect and admiration is extended to my patient husband, Clinton, and children Jacob, Riley, Jasmin, Joy, and Ali. Thank you, also, to Grandma Ruth Riley Jennifer, for her "can do" Boley spirit.

Credits

Boley Historical Museum—interview in person and by phone with curator Henrietta A. Hicks.

Boley Progress, November 1932 account of bank robbery.

Dunbar, Paul Laurence. *Invitation to Love.*

Family Record Accounts—Ruth Riley Jennifer (Boley, OK native).

Johnson, Hannibal B. *Acres of Aspiration: The All-Black Towns in Oklahoma*. Eakin Press, 2002.

Kennedy, Frances H. *Civil War Battlefield Guide-* 2nd ed. Conservation Fund, 1998.

Report of the Adjutant General of the State of Kansas, 1861-65. Topeka, Kansas: 1896 reprint by Alan Russ at www.skyways.lib.ks.us/museums/kng/2kscinfry.html

Stratton, W.K. *Chasing the Rodeo*. New York: Harcourt, Inc., 2005.

Thomas, John D. *Towns of Their Own*. The *New York Times*, February 8, 2004.

Tolson, Arthur L. *Black Oklahomans*. New Orleans: Edwards Printing, 1974.

Wallis, Michael. *Pretty Boy Floyd: Story of Charles Arthur Floyd*. St. Martin Press, 1992.

About the Author

Author Sheila P. Jennifer, wife, mother of five, teacher, and former archivist, writes from her home in Columbia, MD. She is delighted to share this "gem of a story," initially given to her by Boley native Grandma Ruth Riley Jennifer. She encourages all who have access to these buried American stories to dig them up and pass them on to the next generation, so that America's true and inclusive history can enrich us all.

Author's Note

A donation from the book sales of *Back in Boley* will be contributed to assist in the revitalization campaign of the town. Boley is currently working with Langston University (Langston, Oklahoma) towards this end.

Made in the USA
Monee, IL
04 November 2026

67378661R00056